PASSPORT TO SUCCESS

CRIMINAL LAW

Old Bailey Press

OLD BAILEY PRESS LTD
200 Greyhound Road, London W14 9RY

First published 1997

ISBN 1 85836 097 8

British Library Cataloguing-in-Publication.

A CIP Catalogue record for this book is available from the British Library.

Contents

Key to journal abbreviations:

CLJ	Cambridge Law Journal
Crim LR	Criminal Law Review
CLP	Current Legal Problems
ELR	European Law Review
FLJ	Family Law Journal
LQR	Law Quarterly Review
LS	Legal Studies
LTeach	Law Teacher Journal
MLR	Modern Law Review
NLJ	New Law Journal
PL	Public Law

TOPIC 1: Actus Reus and Mens Rea

1. Introduction – elements of a crime

A crime is made up of two elements: actus reus and mens rea. Neither alone is sufficient for criminal liability.

2. Actus reus

The elements of an offence excluding those which concern the mind of the accused.

There are three possible types of actus reus:

a) A positive act

b) A failure to act (omission)

- *R* v *Pittwood* (1902) 19 TLR 37
- *R* v *Instan* [1893] 1 QB 450

c) A state of affairs

- *R* v *Larsonneur* (1933) 149 LT 542

3. Mens rea

The required mental state of the accused

a) The concept of mens rea generally connotes two things:

- that the accused's act was voluntary, and
- that the accused foresaw the consequences of his conduct which in fact occurred.

b) Intention, ie the accused foresaw the consequences of his conduct and it was his purpose to achieve those consequences (direct intent), or he knew that to achieve those consequences he must bring about other forbidden consequences (oblique intent).

Some crimes require a specific or ulterior intent which is to be contrasted with basic intent or mens rea:

- 'Basic intent' is defined by Smith and Hogan as 'intention or recklessness with respect to all those circumstances and consequences of the accused's act (or state of affairs) which constitute the actus reus'.

- 'Specific intent' is sometimes used an an alternative for 'direct' or 'ulterior' intent ie desiring to bring something about, to produce some further consequence beyond the actus reus eg burglary.

Note the terms 'basic intent' and 'specific intent' have particular meanings when used in connection with the defence of intoxication.

- *DPP* v *Majewski* [1977] AC 142

c) Recklessness

Until *MPC* v *Caldwell* [1982] AC 341 recklessness was shown where the accused foresaw the consequences of his act and though not desiring them, he consciously ran the unjustifiable risk of them happening.

- *R* v *Stephenson* [1979] QB 695
- *R* v *Cunningham* [1957] 2 QB 396

The term can also involve an objective element ie where the defendant fails to give thought to a risk that would be obvious to a reasonable man.

- *Caldwell,* above
- *R* v *Lawrence* [1982] AC 510
- *Elliott* v *C* [1983] 1 WLR 939
- *Kong Cheuk Kwan* v *R* (1985) 82 Cr App R 18
- *Chief Constable of Avon and Somerset* v *Shimmen* [1986] Crim LR 800

d) Negligence, ie the accused did not foresee the consequences that have occurred, but the reasonable man would have.

- This is generally not sufficient mens rea for criminal liability.
- Note the distinction between recklessness and negligence has now been blurred by *Caldwell*, above.

e) Blameless inadvertence, ie a reasonable failure to foresee the consequences which have occurred.

f) Transferred malice, ie where D intends harm of a particular type and causes harm of that type, but to an unintended victim or object.

- *R* v *Latimer* (1886) 17 QBD 359
- *R* v *Pembleton* (1874) LR 2 CCR 119
- *Attorney-General's Reference (No 3 of 1994)* [1995] NLJ 1777

g) Where the actus reus is a continuing act or part of a larger transaction, it is sufficient if D has the necessary mens rea during the continuance of the act or during the transaction.

- *Thabo Meli* v *R* [1954] 1 WLR 228
- *R* v *Church* [1966] 1 QB 59
- *Fagan* v *Metropolitan Police Commissioner* [1968] 3 All ER 442
- *R* v *Le Brun* [1991] 3 WLR 653

Sample Questions

1. 'Whilst it is true that not all crimes require full mens rea, it is also true that no crime occurs unless there is an actus reus'.

   Discuss.

2. The golden rule should be that, when directing a jury on the mental element necessary in a crime of specific intent, the judge should avoid any elaboration of what is meant by intent, and leave it to the jury's good sense to decide whether the accused acted with the necessary intent ...' (per Lord Bridge).

   Discuss.

Further Reading

- HLT Textbook Chapter 2
- Horder 'Intention in the Criminal Law' (1995) 58 MCR 678
- Lacey 'Indeterminable Intentions' (1995) 58 MLR 692
- Sullivan 'Cause and the Contemporaneity of Actus Reus and Mens Rea' [1993] CLJ 487

TOPIC 2: Criminal Damage

1. The basic offence: s(1) Criminal Damage Act 1971

D without lawful excuse destroys or damages any property belonging to another intending to destroy or damage it, or being reckless as to such destruction or damage: s1(1) Criminal Damage Act (CDA) 1971.

a) 'Damage' includes a situation where no permanent harm is done.

- *Samuels* v *Stubbs* [1972] 4 SASR 200
- *Morphitis* v *Salmon* [1990] Crim LR 48

b) 'Property' means property of a tangible nature, real or personal including money, wild creatures, which have been tamed or reduced into possession and land.

c) 'Belonging to another' means having custody or control of it, or proprietary interest in it, or having a charge on it: s12(2).

- *R* v *Denton* (1982) 74 Cr App R 81

d) Mens rea

Intention or recklessness as to damage or destruction. Note the meaning of 'reckless'.

- *MPC* v *Caldwell* [1982] AC 341
- *Elliott* v *C* [1983] 1 WLR 939
- *R* v *Sangha* [1988] Crim LR 371
- *R* v *Coles* [1994] Crim LR 820
- *R* v *Merrick* [1995] Crim LR 802

e) D can be liable where he is unaware that he has set in train events which will eventually cause damage yet when he does become so aware he fails to take remedial action.

- *R* v *Miller* [1983] 2 AC 161

2. The 'aggravated' offence – endangering life: s1(2) CDA 1971

Where D without lawful excuse intentionally or recklessly destroys or damages any property, whether belonging to himself or another intending or being reckless as to endangering life of another, he commits an offence under s1(2).

Note *R* v *Steer* [1987] 2 All ER 833; *R* v *Webster* [1995] 2 All ER 168

a) Where D is charged with *recklessly* endangering life the offence is one of basic intent.

- *Caldwell*, above
- *DPP* v *Majewski* [1977] AC 142

b) Where D is charged with intentionally endangering life the offence is one of specific intent.

- *Caldwell*, above

c) Life need not actually be endangered.

- *R* v *Parker* [1993] Crim LR 856

3. Arson: s1(3) CDA 1971

Where an offence under s1 is committed by use of fire the charge is *arson*: s1(3).

4. Other offences under CDA 1971

- Section 2 CDA 1971: involves making threats to destroy or damage another's property or to destroy or damage one's own in a way likely to endanger another's life
- Section 3 CDA 1971: involves having in one's custody or control anything intending it to be used to destroy or damage another's property; or one's own in a way likely to endanger life

5. 'Without lawful excuse'

Section 5 CDA 1971, applies to offences under s1(1) and certain offences under ss2 and 3; subs(2)(a) and (b) set out the situations in which D will be deemed to be acting with lawful excuse based on D's belief in the owner's consent, or acts done in order to protect his own or another's property.

- *R* v *Smith* [1974] QB 354
- *Jaggard* v *Dickinson* [1981] QB 527
- *R* v *Hunt* (1977) 66 Cr App R 105
- *Johnson* v *DPP* [1994] Crim LR 673

Sample Question

Discuss D's possible liability for criminal damage arising in the following circumstances:

a) D lets down the tyres of A's bicycle.

b) D takes A's horse from a field, rides it and then returns it in an exhausted state.

c) D destroys his own painting with a view to claiming against his insurers for its loss.

d) D disconnects the brakes on his own car, knowing that his wife will drive it and hoping that she will be killed. His wife discovers that the brakes have been disconnected before she drives the car.

e) In order to discourage trespassers on his land, D sets traps which cause paint to be sprayed on anyone who activates the trap. A, who is trespassing on the land, sets off a trap and paint is sprayed on his clothing.

Further Reading

- HLT Textbook Chapter 3
- Elliot 'Criminal Damage' [1988] Crim LR 403

TOPIC 3: Non-Fatal Assaults (and Other Offences Against the Person)

1. Assault and battery

a) Assault – an act by D intended to make P apprehend immediate personal violence.

- *Smith* v *Superintendent of Woking Police Station* [1983] Crim LR 323
- *R* v *Lamb* [1967] 2 QB 981
- *R* v *Ireland* [1996] 3 WLR 650 (CA) (nuisance telephone calls where caller remained silent capable of constituting an assault)

b) Battery – actual unlawful infliction of personal violence

c) The term 'assault' is used to cover both as in:

- Section 47 Offences Against the Person Act 1861
- Section 39 Criminal Justice Act 1988
- *R* v *Lynsey* [1995] 3 All ER 654
- *Fagan* v *MPC* [1969] 1 QB 439

d) Words alone can amount to an assault if P is placed in an obviously threatening situation.

- *R* v *Wilson* [1955] 1 All ER 744
- *Read* v *Coker* (1853) 13 CB 850

e) Words may negative an assault.

- *Tuberville* v *Savage* (1669) 2 Keb 545

f) D must intend or be subjectively reckless as to the assault.

- *R* v *Venna* [1975] 3 All ER 788
- *R* v *Cunningham* [1957] 2 QB 396

g) For battery the force need not be applied directly.

- *R* v *Martin* (1881) 8 QBD 54 CCR

2. Defences

a) Consent may be a defence to an assault, including a battery, although there are circumstances where consent will not be a defence.

- *Attorney-General's Reference (No 6 of 1980)* [1981] QB 715
- *R* v *Clarence* (1888) 22 QBD 23
- *R* v *Williams* [1923] 1 KB 340
- *R* v *Donovan* [1934] 2 KB 498
- *R* v *Coney* (1882) 8 QBD 534
- *R* v *Brown* [1993] 2 WLR 556
- *R* v *Wilson* [1996] 3 WLR 125 (CA)

b) An honest mistake as to consent will afford a defence to a charge of assault.

- *R* v *Kimber* [1983] 1 WLR 1118

c) Moderate and reasonable force may be used by parents and teachers to chastise children.

- Section 1 Children and Young Person's Act 1933

d) A defendant may use reasonable force to protect himself and others from the consequences of crime: s3 Criminal Law Act 1967.

3. Section 89 Police Act 1996 (consolidating s51 Police Act 1964)

a) Any person who assaults, resists, or wilfully obstructs a police constable in the execution of his duty, or a person assisting him, shall be guilty of this offence.

b) A police constable is acting in the execution of his duty if his conduct falls within the general scope of preventing crime and catching offenders.

- *R* v *Waterfield* [1964] 1 QB 164
- *Mepstead* v *DPP* [1996] Crim LR 111

c) For assaulting or resisting charges it does not matter whether or not D realises P is a constable.

- *R* v *Forbes & Webb* (1865) 10 Cox CC 362
- *McBride* v *Turnock* [1964] Crim LR 456

d) D must intend an assault or resistance so if he reasonably believes in the existence of facts which justify his act in law, he will be acquitted.

- *R* v *Fennell* [1971] 1 QB 428

e) Obstruction involves more than physical obstruction.

- *Betts* v *Stevens* [1910] 1 KB 1
- *Dibble* v *Ingleton* [1972] 1 QB 480
- *Lewis* v *Cox* [1984] Crim LR 756
- *Hills* v *Ellis* [1983] QB 680

f) The obstruction must be wilful, so D must know it is a policeman.

4. Assault occasioning actual bodily harm

a) This offence is covered by s47 Offences Against the Person Act 1861.

b) The actus reus involves an assault, and the harm must be the natural consequences of the assault.

- *R* v *Roberts* (1971) 56 Cr App R 95

c) Actual bodily harm is any hurt or injury calculated to interfere with the health or comfort of the victim.

- *R* v *Miller* [1954] 2 QB 282
- *R* v *Chan-Fook* [1994] 1 WLR 689

d) The mens rea is that of assault.

- *R* v *Venna* [1976] 1 QB 421

There is no necessity to show foresight of any harm on D's part.

- *R* v *Roberts* (1971) 56 Cr App R 95

- *R* v *Spratt* (1990) 91 Cr App R 362
- *R* v *Savage* [1991] 3 WLR 914

5. **Wounding or inflicting grievous bodily harm**

a) This offence is contained in s20 Offences Against the Person Act 1861.

b) Grievous bodily harm (GBH) means serious bodily harm.

- *DPP* v *Smith* [1961] AC 290
- *R* v *Saunders* [1985] Crim LR 230

c) Wounding requires a breaking of the skin.

- *JJC (A Minor)* v *Eisenhower* [1984] QB 331

d) It is not necessary that the assault be directly inflicted.

- *R* v *Clarence* (1888) 22 QBD 23
- *R* v *Martin* (1881) 8 QBD 54

e) Although a charge of inflicting GBH does not necessarily involve a direct assault, a jury may return a verdict of a lesser offence under s47 if the necessary elements are satisfied.

- *R* v *Wilson* [1983] 3 WLR 686
- *R* v *Mandair* [1994] 2 WLR 700
- *R* v *Burstow* (1996) The Times 30 July (CA) ('stalking')

f) Mens rea 'maliciously'

The defendant must be aware that the natural, probable consequence of his action would be to cause some physical injury to someone.

- *R* v *Mowatt* [1968] 1 QB 421
- *R* v *Sullivan* [1981] Crim LR 46
- *W (A Minor)* v *Dolbey* [1983] Crim LR 681
- *R* v *Savage; R* v *Parmenter* [1991] 3 WLR 914
- Reform proposals: Protection from Harassment Bill 1997

6. **Wounding or causing grievous bodily harm with intent**

a) This offence is contained in s18 Offences Against the Person Act 1861 which contains two distinct crimes:

- wounding or causing GBH with intent to cause GBH;
- wounding or causing GBH with intent to resist lawful apprehension.

b) D must be shown to have intended to cause GBH for the first-mentioned crime (see 6(a) above).

- *R* v *Belfon* [1976] 1 WLR 741
- *R* v *Bryson* [1985] Crim LR 669

c) 'Cause' is a wider term than 'inflict' and would probably cover conduct such as that in *R* v *Clarence*, above, subject to D's mens rea.

d) Note the meaning of 'maliciously' (see 5(f) above), particularly in the context of second-mentioned crime (see 6(a) above).

7. **Administering poison**

a) This is an offence under s23 and s24 Offences Against the Person Act 1861.

b) Both involve the administration of a poison or obnoxious thing.

- *R* v *Marcus* [1981] 1 WLR 774
- *R* v *Gillard* (1988) 87 Cr App R 189

c) Under s23 the actus reus includes an additional element ie so as to thereby endanger life or to inflict GBH.

d) The s23 offence may be committed recklessly, and no mens rea is required as to the second part of the actus reus.

- *R* v *Cunningham* [1957] 2 QB 396
- *R* v *Cato* [1976] 1 WLR 110

e) Section 24 requires specific intent, namely to injure, aggrieve or annoy.

- *R* v *Wetherall* [1968] Crim LR 115
- *R* v *Hill* [1986] Crim LR 815

8. False imprisonment

a) Involves the detention of another who must be totally cut off from escape, and it is probable that the victim need not realise he is being detained.

b) Detention may be lawful in some circumstances eg under a valid arrest warrant.

9. Kidnap

This offence is an aggravated form of false imprisonment and involves the stealing and carrying away of a person from a place where he wishes to be. If the victim goes willingly there is no offence.

10. Bigamy

a) It is an offence contrary to s57 OAPA 1861 to marry someone during the life of a former spouse while that first marriage still subsists.

b) If the first marriage is void no offence is committed. Where the first marriage is voidable, a second marriage during its subsistence will amount to bigamy.

Note:

- *R* v *Sarwan Singh* [1962] 3 All ER 612
- *R* v *Sagoo* [1975] QB 885

c) D has a defence if he has not seen or heard from his spouse for seven years.

- *R* v *Faulkes* (1903) 19 TLR 250

d) Mens rea involves more than an intention go to through a marriage ceremony.

- *R* v *Tolson* (1889) 23 QBD 168
- *R* v *King* [1964] 1 QB 285

11. Rape

a) Section 41 Criminal Justice and Public Order Act 1994 amends the old definition of rape contained in s1 Sexual Offences (Amendment) Act 1976 to effectively provide, for the first time in English law, that a man may be guilty of raping another man. The new definition of rape is as follows:

'a man commits rape if:

- he has sexual intercourse with a person (whether vaginal or anal) who at the time of the intercourse does not consent to it; and
- at the time he knows that the person does not consent to the intercourse or is reckless as to whether that person consents to it.'

b) Intercourse is deemed complete upon proof of penetration (s44 Sexual Offences Act 1956), but note it is a continuing act so that where a woman initially gives her consent to the intercourse but withdraws consent during intercourse, rape is committed if D continues the intercourse realising her consent to have been withdrawn.

c) A man can be convicted of rape of his wife.

- *R* v *R* [1991] 3 WLR 767 HL

d) Fraud as to the nature of the act itself can vitiate consent.

- *R* v *Williams* [1923] 1 KB 340
- *R* v *Papadimitropoulas* (1957) 98 CLR 249
- *R* v *Linekar* [1995] 2 WLR 237
- *R* v *Elbekkay* [1995] Crim LR 163

e) Mens rea is intention or subjective recklessness as to non-consensual sexual intercourse with a woman.

- *R* v *Satnam and Kewal* (1983) 78 Cr App R 149

Sample Questions

1. Student A called student B a nitwit and in response B picked up a board rubber and threw it in A's direction intending to miss him but hoping that it would give him a fright and stip him from insulting him again. The board rubber hit A on the forehead causing a deep cut requiring treatment in the outpatients department of the local hospital.

   Advise B as to his criminal liability, if any.

   Would it make any difference to your answer if:

   a) B had intended to hit A on the head with the board rubber but as it was quite light thought it would cause no injury?

   b) B had intended to hit A on the head hoping to cause him a bump on the head?

2. E was playing squash with F when E hit F in the eye with a squash racquet when he was reaching for the ball. As a result F was rendered unconscious and lost his eye. When G, F's father, heard of the accident he telephoned E and said, 'I'll be in London in nine months' time. I will visit you and give you a good hiding'. E was very worried by this threat.

   Advise E and G.

Further Reading

- HLT Textbook Chapters 4 and 5
- Criminal Law Revision Committee, 14th Report on offences against the person
- Law Commission Consultation Paper No 134 (1994) on consent and offences against the person
- Kell 'Psychiatric Injury and the Bodily Harm Criteria' (1995) 111 LQR 27
- Ormerod 'Law Commission Consultation Paper' (1994) 57 MLR 928

TOPIC 4: Homicide: Murder and Manslaughter

1. Homicide

Homicide is the killing of another. If it is unlawful it is either murder or manslaughter depending on the accused's state of mind.

2. Causation

Whichever type of homicide is charged, it must be proved that the accused caused the death. The old rule that death must occur within a year and a day of the accused's act has been abolished by the Law Reform (Year and a Day Rule) Act 1996

a) Whether or not the accused's act is the cause of death is a mixed question of fact and law. Whether or not an intervening event can be said to be the cause of death is primarily a question of law.

- *R* v *Smith* [1959] 2 QB 35
- *R* v *Jordan* (1956) 40 Cr App R 152
- *R* v *Blaue* [1975] 1 WLR 1411
- *R* v *Malcherek; R* v *Steel* [1981] 2 All ER 422
- *R* v *Cheshire* (1991) 93 Cr App R 251
- *R* v *Dawson* (1985) 81 Cr App R 150
- *R* v *Mellor* (1996) 2 Cr App R 245

b) D will be liable where he puts P into a position where P risks his life to escape from apprehended harm from D

- *R* v *Mackie* (1973) 57 Cr App R 453
- *R* v *Roberts* (1971) 56 Cr App R 95
- *R* v *Williams* [1992] 1 WLR 380
- *R* v *Corbett* [1996] Crim LR 594

or where the fear he creates in another causes their death.

- *R* v *Pagett* (1983) 76 Cr App R 279
- *R* v *Dear* [1996] Crim LR 595

3. Murder

a) For the actus reus – see above

b) Mens rea

The law of foresight and intention 1961-1990

- *DPP* v *Smith* [1961] AC 290 HL:

  A person (if sane and sober) is presumed to have intended 'natural and probable consequences' of any voluntary act which he has 'aimed at someone'. It is not necessary for the prosecution to prove that he actually foresaw or intended that consequence.

- Section 8 Criminal Justice Act 1967:

  A person is not to be presumed to have 'intended' or to have foreseen a consequence of his actions 'by reason only of its being a natural and probable consequence of those actions' but this question must be decided subjectively. The effect of s8 is to overrule *DPP* v *Smith*, above.

- A direction to a jury which might lead them to suppose that a defendant is guilty merely because ordinary people in his position would have foreseen the consequences of his actions is a wrong direction.

- *Hyam* v *DPP* [1975] AC 55 HL:

  Whether or not disregarding actual foresight of probable consequences is the same thing, in law, as intending those consequences, a person will be guilty of murder if he or she makes a *decision* to expose another person to the 'highly probable risk' of death or GBH, and death is caused by this conduct. Lord Hailsham thought that it was the defendant's decision which amounted to an intention in law, not mere 'foresight' as such. Lord Dilhorne and Lord Cross thought that foresight alone was enough, even if it did *not* amount to a form of 'intention'. Lord Diplock and Lord

Kilbrandon thought that only foresight as to *death* was sufficient for a charge of murder, not foresight as to GBH – but they both thought that foresight of 'highly probable' consequences *was* a form of intention. (Note: It is therefore difficult to extract the ratio decidendi from this case.)

- *DPP* v *Majewski* [1977] AC 142 HL:

  Section 8 CJA 1967 explains *how* intention or foresight is to be proved – not *when* it has to be proved. Accordingly, there is no obligation on the prosecution to prove that a drunken person knew what he was doing when he committed assault or any other offence of 'basic intent'. But his drunkenness would be a defence to murder, theft, and any other offence of 'specific intent' if he was too intoxicated to have formed that intent or if, for any other reason, he did not actually form that intent. Rape is a crime of basic intent.

- *R* v *Cunningham* [1982] AC 566 HL:

  A person will be guilty of murder if he intended to cause GBH and death resulted. *R* v *Vickers* [1957] 2 QB 664 was correctly decided.

- The 41st edition of Archbold's *Pleading, Evidence and Practice in Criminal Cases* was published 1982 (1st edn published in 1822). It continues to give the following definition of 'intention' and to claim that it 'is in accordance with the great preponderance of authority':

  'In law a man intends the consequences of his voluntary act:

  – when he desires it to happen, whether or not he foresees that it probably will happen; or

  – when he foresees that it will probably happen, whether he desires it or not.'

- *R* v *Moloney* [1985] AC 905 HL:

  The House of Lords held that (b) of the above definition is wrong. The fact that a defendant foresees a consequence is only evidence that he *may* have intended it. If the consequence was a 'natural' consequence of the defendant's conduct the jury are entitled to infer that he foresaw it, and if he actually foresaw it, they are entitled to infer that he intended it, but neither of these inferences is automatic. The correct test is:

> 'if the prosecution prove an act the natural consequences of which would be a certain result and no evidence or explanation is given, then a jury may, on a proper direction, find that the prisoner is guilty of doing the act with the intent alleged, but if on the totality of the evidence there is room for more than one view as to the intent of the prisoner, the prisoner is entitled to be acquitted.'

(*Hyam* v *DPP* not overruled, but nevertheless superseded?)

- *R* v *Hancock and Shankland* [1986] AC 455 HL:

  In this case, the House of Lords held that *R* v *Moloney*, above did not go far enough. It is not enough that the consequence in question was a 'natural' consequence. Before the jury are entitled to infer that the defendant foresaw this consequence (and may, therefore, have intended it also), the consequence in question must be proved to be 'natural and probable'. 'Natural' merely implies that there was cause and effect. 'Probable' shows that the risk of the consequence was a high one.

- *R* v *Nedrick* [1986] 1 WLR 1025 CA:

  The combined effect of *R* v *Moloney* above and *R* v *Hancock and Shankland* above is that a jury is not entitled to infer that the defendant intended a particular consequence unless that consequence was certain to result, 'barring some unforeseen intervention' and the defendant recognised this also.

  (Note: This degree of inevitability need not be the case if there is some *direct* evidence of the defendant's intentions, eg written or spoken threats before the crime; or things said at the time of committing the crime; or a confession made after the crime.)

- *R* v *Walker & Hayles* [1990] Crim LR 44 CA:

  On a charge of attempted murder the jury had not been misdirected when told they could convict if they were sure the appellants intended to kill in the sense that they were sure that the appellants knew that there was a 'very high degree of probability' that the victim would be killed.

  (Note: The Court of Appeal did suggest that in those rare cases where a direction on intention with reference to foresight was required, the courts should continue to use 'virtual certainty' as the test rather than 'high probability'.)

4. Manslaughter

The actus reus is the same as for murder. Note that there are two types of manslaughter:

- Voluntary – where the requirements of murder are satisfied, but D falls within an accepted defence
- Involuntary – where there is a culpable taking of human life without malice aforethought

Voluntary manslaughter

a) Provocation

Where there is evidence that D was provoked by things done, or said, or by both together, to lose his self control the jury shall decide whether the provocation was enough to make a reasonable man do as D did.

- Section 3 Homicide Act 1957
- *R* v *Acott* [1996] 4 All ER 443 (subject to appeal to HL)
- *R* v *Duffy* [1949] 1 All ER 932

There are two questions to consider:

1. Was D provoked into losing his self control? – a subjective question
   - *R* v *Hayward* (1833) 6 C and P 157
   - *R* v *Ibrams and Gregory* [1982] Crim LR 229
   - *R* v *Pearson* [1992] Crim LR 193

2. Would a reasonable man have lost his self control in similar circumstances and have done what D did? – an objective question
   - *DPP* v *Camplin* [1978] AC 705
   - *Luc Thiet Thuan* v *R* [1996] 2 All ER 1033 (PC)
   - *R* v *Dryden* [1995] 4 All ER 897
   - *R* v *Raven* [1982] Crim LR 51
   - *R* v *Humphries* [1995] NLJ 1032
   - *Mancini* v *DPP* [1942] AC 1
   - *R* v *Thornton* (1995) The Times 14 December
   - *R* v *Ali* [1989] Crim LR 736
   - *R* v *Morhall* [1995] 3 WLR 330

   Note the effect of mistake and drunkenness
   - *Albert* v *Lavin* [1981] 1 All ER 628
   - *R* v *Wardrope* [1960] Crim LR 770

b) Diminished responsibility

- Where D was suffering from such abnormality of mind as substantially impaired his mental responsibilities
  - Section 2 Homicide Act 1957
  - *R* v *Byrne* [1960] 2 QB 396
  - *R* v *Seers* [1985] Crim LR 85
  - *R* v *Gittens* [1984] QB 698
  - *R* v *Fenton* (1975) 61 Cr App R 261
  - *R* v *Sanderson* (1994) 98 Cr App R 325
- Note the effect of drunkenness
  - *R* v *Atkinson* [1985] Crim LR 314
  - *R* v *Tandy* [1989] 1 All ER 267
  - *R* v *Egan* [1992] 4 All ER 470

c) Infanticide

Where a woman, by act or omission causes the death of her child under the age of 12 months, but at that time the balance of her mind was disturbed by reason of her not having fully recovered from the effect of giving birth.

- Section 1 Infanticide Act 1938

d) Suicide pact

It is manslaughter, and not murder where a person kills another in pursuance of a suicide pact, ie a common agreement between two or more people, having for its object the death of all of them.

- Section 4 Homicide Act 1957

Note: a person who aids, abets, counsels or procures the suicide or attempted suicide of another commits an offence under s2 Suicide Act 1961.

- *Attorney-General* v *Able* [1984] QB 795

Involuntary manslaughter

There are two main categories: constructive manslaughter and reckless manslaughter, although where the court is satisfied that D caused the death by one or other of two or more acts it is not necessary to prove which acts caused the death.

a) Constructive manslaughter

The defendant must intend to commit an unlawful act which must be objectively dangerous and which must be the cause of the victim's death: *R* v *Dawson* (1985) 81 Cr App R 150; *R* v *Goodfellow* (1986) 83 Cr App R 23.

- The act must be unlawful and probably be a crime
  - *R* v *Fenton* (1830) 1 Lew CC 179
  - *R* v *Franklin* (1883) 15 Cox CC 163
- It must be unlawful in itself and not because of the negligent manner in which it is performed, and it must be positive.
  - *Andrews* v *DPP* [1937] AC 576

- D must intend to commit the unlawful act.
  - *R* v *Lamb* [1967] 2 All ER 1282
- It was thought that the act had to be aimed at someone: *R* v *Dalby* [1982] 1 WLR 425. However, it is now established that this is not so and that the Dalby case was concerned with establishing causation and not an additional condition for constructive manslaughter.
  - *R* v *Mitchell* [1983] 2 WLR 938
  - *R* v *Goodfellow* [1986] Crim LR 468
- The act must be likely, according to objective standards, to cause some physical harm, albeit not serious harm.
  - *R* v *Church* [1966] 1 QB 59
  - *DPP* v *Newbury and Jones* [1976] AC 500
  - *R* v *Larkin* [1943] 1 All ER 217
  - *R* v *Dawson*, above

b) Reckless manslaughter

- Until recently this head was known as manslaughter due to gross negligence. However, defining this head of manslaughter was virtually impossible. It was described as negligence going beyond a mere matter of compensation between subjects and showing such disregard for life and safety of others as to amount to a crime.
  - *R* v *Bateman* [1925] All ER 45
- It was often equated with recklessness although there was confusion as to whether this was an objective or subjective recklessness.
  - *R* v *Stone & Dobinson* [1977] 2 All ER 341
  - *R* v *Bateman*, above
  - *Andrews* v *DPP*, above

- More recently it has been equated with recklessness in an objective sense, as enunciated in *Caldwell*, above and *R* v *Lawrence* [1982] AC 510.
  - *R* v *Seymour* [1983] 2 AC 493
  - *Kong Cheuk Kwan* v *R* (1985) 82 Cr App R 18
- The resurrection of manslaughter by gross negligence.
  - *R* v *Adomako* [1994] 3 WLR 288
  - Reform proposals: Law Commission report no 237 (May 1996)

c) Killing recklessly

Authority for this head of manslaughter is slight and it is based on a *subjective* recklessness.

5. Lawful homicide

If D is able to bring himself within one of the recognised defences, his homicide would cease to be unlawful.

a) Killing while preventing crime or arresting offenders

Involves the use of reasonable force to prevent crime or effect or assist in a lawful arrest of offenders.

- Section 3 Criminal Law Act 1967

b) Self defence

This would undoubtedly also be covered under s3 CLA 1967. However, there is still a common law right of self-defence.

- *R* v *Duffy* [1967] 1 QB 63
- *R* v *Clegg* [1995] 2 WLR 80

c) Defence of property

Section 3 could also apply here, although it would rarely do so where death has resulted, as killing can seldom be justified. A most likely example would be a burglar who is assaulted – what would otherwise be constructive manslaughter would become lawful homicide if reasonable force was used.

6. Killing an unborn child

Two offences apply here: child destruction under the Infant Life Preservation Act 1929, and attempting to procure a miscarriage under the Offences Against the Person Act 1861.

a) Child destruction

- Involves the intentional destruction of a child capable of being born alive. It seems that 'capable of being born alive' means capable of surviving at birth, and a foetus of less than 24 weeks gestation, at current medical standards, would not be deemed capable of surviving birth.
  - *C* v *S* [1987] 2 WLR 1108
- The Abortion Act 1967 does not apply to this offence. However, s1(1) Infant Life Preservation Act 1929 provides that there shall be no offence if it is proved that the act which caused the death of the child was done in good faith to preserve the life of the mother.
  - *R* v *Bourne* [1939] 1 KB 687

b) Attempt to procure a miscarriage. The offence is committed in two ways:

- A pregnant woman, who with intent to procure a miscarriage, unlawfully administers to herself a poison or noxious substance, or unlawfully uses any instrument or other means with such intent, shall be guilty.
- Any other person who with intent to procure the miscarriage of any woman, whether she is pregnant or not, unlawfully administers to her a poison or noxious substance, or unlawfully uses any instrument or other means on her with such intent, shall be guilty.
  - Section 58 Offences Against the Person Act 1861
  - *R* v *Marcus* [1981] 1 WLR 774
- Note if the woman herself is charged, she must be or have been pregnant, but this is not so if anyone else is charged, although a non-pregnant woman may be

guilty of conspiracy and aiding and abetting another to commit the offence.

- *R* v *Whitchurch* (1890) 24 QBD 420
- *R* v *Sockett* (1908) 72 JP 428

- A defence to the charge is provided in the Abortion Act 1967:
  - If the pregnancy is terminated before 24 weeks by a registered medical practitioner where two registered medical practitioners are of the opinion, formed in good faith, that the continuance of the pregnancy would involve risk to the mother's life or of injury to her health, or the health of her existing children greater than if the pregnancy were terminated, or that there is a substantial risk of the child being born seriously handicapped.
  - There are other requirements eg the operation must be performed in an approved clinic, although such requirements need not be fulfilled in emergency cases.
- Note the offence of supplying or procuring a poison or noxious substance, or any instrument or other means intending it to be used to procure a miscarriage.
  - Section 59 Offences Against the Person Act 1861

7. Threats to kill

A person who without lawful excuse threatens to kill another, or a third party, intending the other to fear it would be carried out shall be guilty of an offence.

- Section 16 Offences Against the Person Act 1861

Sample Questions

1. Donald was awaiting the arrival of two friends, Mick and Jason. When they entered his room, Donald, as a practical joke, pulled out an imitation gun and pointed it at them. Unknown to Donald, Mick suffered from a heart disease. The shock Mick suffered caused him to collapse and die. Jason was

also shocked and scared by Donald's behaviour and jumped out of the window, falling some fifteen feet. He suffered serious injuries. The experience made Jason very depressed and nervous. He became unwilling to eat. He was visited every day by his only friend, Nigel, who used to feed Jason. Nigel went on holiday without telling anyone of his plan. Nigel believed, quite wrongly, that Jason would be able to look after himself. In fact Jason died of starvation while Nigel was away.

Advise Donald and Nigel as to their criminal liability, if any.

2. Dunk, a bad-tempered old soldier, was wounded while on active service and now has a wooden leg. One evening, while Dunk is drinking in a public house, he notices that one of the other customers is Vogue. Dunk erroneously believes that Vogue has assaulted Dunk's daughter. Dunk limps over to where Vogue is sitting and says: 'If you touch my daughter again I'll castrate you'. Dunk emphasises this remark by producing a large pair of scissors and making snipping movements in the vicinity of his own stomach. Vogue replies: 'I wouldn't touch your daughter with a barge pole, she's an ugly old slag and I'm not afraid of an old cowardly cripple'.

   Vogue picks up an empty glass, smashes the rim and stands up pointing the jagged glass in a threatening manner towards Dunk. Dunk, enraged by Vogue's remarks and fearing that Vogue is about to attack him, lunges at Vogue with the scissors, fatally stabbing Vogue in the heart.

   Advise Dunk, who has been charged with the murder of Vogue.

Further Reading

- HLT Textbook Chapters 6, 7 and 8
- Law Commission Consultation Paper No 135 on involuntary manslaughter (1994)
- Briggs 'Provocation Re-Reassessed' (1996) 112 LQR 403
- Gardner 'Causation in Homicide' (1992) 108 LQR 24
- Gardner 'Manslaughter by Gross Negligence: *R* v *Adomako*' (1995) 111 LQR 22
- Horder 'Provocation and Loss of Self-control' (1992) 108 LQR 191

- Horder 'Provocation's Reasonable Man Reassessed' (1996) 112 LQR 35
- Leigh 'Liability for Inadvertence: *R* v *Adomako*' (1995) 58 MLR 457
- McColgan 'Involuntary Manslaughter' [1994] Crim LR 547
- Padfield 'Why does Provocation Diminish Culpability?' [1996] CLJ 420
- Phillips '*R* v *Adomako*; Is this the final word on negligent manslaughter?' (1995) 29 LTeach 338
- Virgo 'Back to Basics: Reconstructing Manslaughter' [1994] CLJ 44
- Virgo 'Reconstructing Manslaughter' [1995] CLJ 14
- Wasik 'Law of Involuntary Manslaughter' [1994] Crim LR 883
- WIlson 'A Plea for Rationality in the Law of Murder' (1991) 10 307

TOPIC 5: Participation

1. Principal offender

A principal offender is one who commits the actus reus or who secures its commission through an innocent agent.

- *R* v *Michael* (1840) 9 C and P 356

2. Aiding, abetting, counselling or procuring

A person who aids, abets, counsels or procures the commission of an offence is to be treated as a principal offender for the purposes of trial and punishment.

- Section 8 Accessories and Abettors Act 1861

For the meaning of the terms see:

- *AG's Reference (No 1 of 1975)* [1975] QB 773

3. Aider and abettor

An aider and abettor is present at the scene of the crime and gives active encouragement or assistance to the principal.

- *R* v *Coney* (1882) 8 QBD 534
- *R* v *Clarkson* [1971] 1 WLR 1402

a) He must know the facts which constitute the crime.

- *Johnson* v *Youden* [1950] 1 KB 544
- *Callow* v *Tillstone* (1900) 83 LT 411

b) Each party is liable for acts done in pursuance of a joint enterprise, and for any accidental consequence arising from its execution.

- *R* v *Betts & Ridley* (1930) 22 Cr App R 148
- *R* v *Lovesey & Peterson* (1969) 53 Cr App R 461
- *R* v *Roberts* (1993) 96 Cr App R 291
- *Chan Wing-Sui and Others* v *R* [1984] 3 All ER 871; [1985] AC 168 (PC)
- *R* v *Bamborough* [1996] Crim LR 744

- *R* v *Hyde, Sunsex and Collins* [1990] 3 WLR 1115
- *R* v *Stewart and Schofield* (1995) 1 Cr App R 41

4. Counsellor and procurer

A counsellor and procurer is one who before a crime is committed advises its commission or gives other assistance to the principal. An incitor or conspirator would be guilty of counselling if the offence was committed.

a) Where D counsels the commission of a *particular crime* he is guilty even though it is committed in a different way from that counselled.

- *R* v *Saunders & Archer* (1573) 2 Plowd 473
- *R* v *Calhaem* [1985] 2 All ER 266
- *R* v *Leahy* [1985] Crim LR 99

b) Where D counsels a *particular type of crime* he is guilty of any crime of that type committed as a result of his counsel.

- *R* v *Bainbridge* [1959] 3 WLR 356

D must intend the crime counselled to be committed, although indifference will suffice.

- *NCB* v *Gamble* [1959] QB 11

For 'procuring' D must intend the crime to be committed.

- *Blakely, Sutton* v *DPP* [1991] Crim LR 763

5. Defences

a) Withdrawal

D will have a defence if he withdraws before the contemplated crime is committed, although his liability for incitement or conspiracy will be unaffected.

- *R* v *Becerra and Cooper* (1975) 62 Cr App R 212
- *R* v *Grundy* [1977] Crim LR 543
- *R* v *Whitefield* [1984] Crim LR 97

b) No principal actus reus

If the actus reus of the principal offence has not been committed there can be no accomplice: *Thornton* v *Mitchell* [1940] 1 All ER 339

- Distinguish a case of no actus reus from a case where there is an actus reus, but no principal offender eg because he has a defence or the prosecution cannot prove who the principal offender is.
  - *R* v *Bourne* (1952) 36 Cr App R 125
  - *R* v *Cogan and Leak* [1976] QB 217
  - *Hui Chi-Ming* v *R* [1991] 3 WLR 495
  - *R* v *Hyde* [1990] 3 WLR 1115
- An accomplice may be convicted even though s/he could not commit the offence as a principal.
- A victim who is specifically protected cannot aid an offence against himself or herself.
  - *R* v *Tyrrell* [1894] 1 QB 710

6. Impeding arrest

a) Where a person has committed an arrestable offence, any other person knowing or believing him to be guilty of the offence, or another arrestable offence, who unlawfully does any act with intent to impede his arrest or prosecution shall be guilty of an offence.

- Section 4(1) Criminal Law Act 1967

b) Where a person has committed an arrestable offence, any other person who, knowing or believing that the offence or other arrestable offence has been committed, and that he has information which might be of material assistance in securing the prosecution or conviction of an offender for it, accepts or agrees to accept for not disclosing that information any consideration other than the making good of loss or injury caused by the offence or the making of reasonable compensation for such loss or injury shall be liable.

- Section 5(1) Criminal Law Act 1967

Sample Questions

1. Philip persuades Sarah to join him in a robbery. The plan is to way-lay a shopkeeper as he is taking money to pay into a bank. Philip is to snatch the bag from the victim while Sarah keeps watch a yard or so away and prevents interference from passers-by. On the morning of the event, Sarah says to Philip 'don't rough him up too much' to which Philip replies 'OK, but I may have to knock him out'. The following day Sarah and Philip follow the shopkeeper on his way to the bank and in a quiet street Philip runs up to him and grabs his bag. The shopkeeper struggles to escape, but Philip knocks him down and wrenches the bag from his grasp. Philip and Sarah then start to run away, but Philip, hearing the victim shout for help, runs back, pulls out a cosh and beats him severely on the head with it. The shopkeeper dies as a result of this beating.

   Advise Philip and Sarah as to their criminal liability, if any.

2. Len gets involved in a fight with another man in a public house. The police are called and Len is warned that he may be prosecuted for assault. Two days later, Len is visited by Stephen, a man he does not know, but who witnessed the fight. Stephen tells Len that in return for £200 he will come forward as a witness for the defence, if Len is prosecuted, and testify that Len was attacked first and only acted in self-defence. Len tells Stephen that he will accept his offer, but he reports Stephen's conduct to the police.

   Is Stephen liable to prosecution?

Further Reading

- HLT Textbook Chapters 9 and 10
- Law Commission Consultation Paper No 131 (1993): *Assisting and Encouraging Crime*
- Padfield 'The High Price of Participation in Criminal Activities' [1993] CLJ 373

TOPIC 6: Inchoate Offences: Incitement, Conspiracy and Attempt

1. Incitement

a) It is a common law offence to incite another to commit an indictable or summary offence.

b) D must urge or spur on by advice, encouragement, persuasion, threats or pressure.

- *Race Relations Board* v *Applin* [1973] QB 815

c) The incitement must reach the incitee's mind, if it does not there may be an attempt.

- *R* v *Ransford* (1874) 31 LT 488

d) It need not be aimed at a particular person.

- *R* v *Most* (1881) 7 QBD 244

e) D should intend that the offence incited be committed and have knowledge of, or be recklessness as to, the facts necessary to make the conduct incited an offence.

- *Invicta Plastics Ltd* v *Clare* [1976] Crim LR 131

f) It seems that the question of impossibility in incitement is governed by *Haughton* v *Smith* [1975] AC 476.

- *R* v *Fitzmaurice* [1983] 2 WLR 227

g) The act incited must be one which when done by the person incited would be a crime.

- *R* v *Curr* [1968] 2 QB 944
- *R* v *Whitehouse* [1977] QB 868

h) When the offence incited is committed the incitor becomes a party to the full offence (as a counsellor/procurer).

i) Under statute: Sexual offences (Conspiracy and Incitement) Act 1996 removes any bar to prosecution based on an assertion that the acts encouraged or agreed upon would take place beyond the jurisdiction of the English courts.

2. Conspiracy

Common Law

At common law conspiracy is an agreement between two or more persons to effect an unlawful purpose. The Criminal Law Act 1977 preserves the common law offences of conspiracy to defraud, to corrupt public morals and to outrage public decency.

a) *To defraud*

- An agreement to carry out a course of conduct that would be dishonest, but would not necessarily involve the commission of a substantive offence.
  - *R* v *Allsop* (1976) 64 Cr App R 29
  - *R* v *Hollingshead* [1985] AC 975
  - *Wai Yutsang* v *R* [1991] 3 WLR 1006
  - *Adams* v *R* [1995] 1 WLR 52
- Where the performance of the agreement would involve the commission of a substantive offence the conspiracy could be charged under s1 Criminal Law Act 1977 or as a common law conspiracy to defraud.
  - Section 12 Criminal Justice Act 1987

b) *Corruption of public morals* '... conduct which a jury might find destructive to the very fabric of society.'

- *Shaw* v *DPP* [1962] AC 220
- *Knuller* v *DPP* [1972] AC 435

c) *Outraging public decency* '... goes considerably beyond offending the susceptibilities of, or even shocking, reasonable people ... [it is] concerned with recognising minimum standards of decency, which are likely to vary from time to time.'

- *Knuller* v *DPP*, above

Statutory conspiracy

An agreement between two or more persons to pursue a course of conduct, which if carried out in accordance with their intentions, either will necessarily involve the commission of any offence by one or more parties to the agreement, or would do so but for the existence of facts which render the commission of the offence impossible.

- Section 1(1) Criminal Law Act 1977 as amended by
- Section 5(1) Criminal Attempts Act 1981

a) Agreement – there must be more than mere negotiations

b) Two or more persons

  - Note s2(2) Criminal Law Act 1977

c) Any offence

  - A crime, summary or indictable
  - The agreement must necessarily involve the commission of an offence.
  - Parties entering England intending to carry out an agreement concluded abroad are triable here.
    - *DPP* v *Doot* [1973] AC 807

d) Impossibility

  - *Physical impossibility* due to ineptitude or to the object not being there will not be a defence to a charge of conspiracy.
  - *Legal impossibility* will not be a defence.
    - *R* v *Shivpuri* [1987] AC 1

e) Mens rea

The parties must intend to pursue a course of conduct which will necessarily amount to the commission of an offence if the agreement is carried out in accordance with their intentions.

  - *R* v *Anderson* [1986] AC 27
  - *Yip Chiu-cheung* v *R* [1994] 3 WLR 514 PC

f) Sexual Offences (Conspiracy and Incitement) Act 1996, above

3. Attempt

Actus reus

a) The act must be more than merely preparatory to the commission of the offence.

- Section 1(1) Criminal Attempts Act 1981
- *R* v *Widdowson* [1986] Crim LR 233

Earlier case law *may* still be relevant, but be cautious.

- *R* v *Robinson* [1915] 2 KB 342
- *R* v *Button* [1900] 2 QB 597
- *Comer* v *Bloomfield* (1970) 55 Cr App R 305
- *R* v *Eagleton* (1855) Dears CCR 515

Now note:

- *R* v *Jones* (1990) 91 Cr App R 351
- *R* v *Gullefer* (1990) 91 Cr App R 356
- *R* v *Campbell* (1991) 93 Cr App R 350
- *R* v *Geddes* (1996) The Times 16 July (CA)

b) Impossibility

- Physical impossibility due to ineptitude or to the subject not being there will not be a defence.
  - Section 1(2) Criminal Attempts Act 1981
- Legal impossibility is not a defence
  - *R* v *Shivpuri* [1987] AC 1

c) If all the elements of the attempt exist, the accused's voluntary withdrawal from committing the offence is no defence.

- *R* v *Taylor* (1859) 1 F & F 511

Mens rea

a) D must intend to commit the full offence.

b) Where the definition of the full offence requires a consequence the accused must intend that consequence.

- *R* v *Mohan* [1976] QB 1
- *R* v *Pearmon* (1985) 80 Cr App R 259
- *R* v *Walker & Hayles* (1990) 90 Cr App R 226

c) For attempted murder the mens rea is intention to kill.

- *R* v *Whybrow* (1951) 35 Cr App R 141

d) There is some doubt as to whether mens rea is required where the offence attempted is one of strict liability.

e) The intent required for attempt may be classed as specific intent for the purposes of the intoxication defence.

Sample Question

On Monday, John and Peter agree to steal Victor's car radio and his Matisse painting, if Victor is not at home. Unknown to John and Peter, Victor removed both articles on the preceding Sunday and lent them to a friend. John and Peter go to Victor's house and ring the door-bell. No-one replies. As they are about to force open a window, Peter suggests that instead they take the radio first. John agrees. They go to Victor's car and, as they are about to open the door, discover that the radio has been removed. They are then arrested by a policeman who has been observing them throughout.

Discuss the criminal liability of John and Peter.

Further Reading

- HLT Textbook Chapters 11 and 12
- Duff 'The Circumstances of an Attempt' [1991] CLJ 100
- Smith 'Proximity in Attempt: Lord Lane's Midway Course' [1991] Crim LR 576
- Williams 'Wrong Turnings on the Law of Attempt' [1991] Crim LR 416

TOPIC 7: General Defences

1. Infancy

a) If D is under 10 there is an irrebuttable presumption that he is incapable of committing any crime.

- Section 16 Children and Young Persons Act 1933

b) A child aged between 10–14 is presumed to be doli incapax but this presumption can be rebutted by showing that the child had 'mischievous discretion' *JM* v *Runeckles* (1984) 79 Cr App R 255 and confirmed in *C* v *DPP* [1995] 2 WLR 383 HL.

c) Persons of 14 or over are subject to full responsibility for their acts.

d) Note, males under 14 are irrebutably presumed to be incapable of committing crimes involving sexual potency as a principal offender, although they may be guilty as accomplices.

2. Insanity

a) A successful plea will result in D's incarceration in a hospital for an indefinite period. The verdict is 'not guilty by reason of insanity'.

b) There are three stages at which it may be established although it is only a 'defence' at the third stage.

Before the accused is brought to trial: Home Secretary on advice of at least two medical practitioners that D is suffering from mental illness or severe subnormality may commit him to a hospital if he does not consider it practicable to bring D to trial.

- Mental Health Act 1959

Before the commencement of the trial: when D may be found unfit to plead.

- Criminal Procedure (Insanity) Act 1964

At the trial: the 'defence' of legal insanity at the time of the offence.

- The law is governed by the *M'Naghten* rules (1843) 10 Cl and F 210 which provide that everyone is presumed sane until the contrary is proved on the balance of probabilities.
- Note the test set out in the *M'Naghten* rules
- Defect of reason: connotes D was deprived of reasoning powers
- Disease of mind: a legal question, not a medical one
  - *R* v *Quick* [1973] QB 910
  - *R* v *Kemp* [1956] 3 All ER 249
  - *R* v *Sullivan* [1984] AC 156
- Nature and quality: refers to physical nature of the act
- Wrong: includes legally wrong
  - *R* v *Windle* [1952] 2 QB 826

3. Non-insane automatism

a) All conduct must be 'willed' and where the Crown cannot prove that D's act was willed the defence is automatism eg sleepwalking.

b) The defence does not apply where automatism arises:

- From a disease of the mind – the correct defence there is insanity
  - *R* v *Quick*, above
  - *R* v *Burgess* (1991) 93 Cr App R 41
  - *R* v *Sullivan* [1984] AC 156
  - *R* v *T* [1990] Crim LR 256
- Where the accused's act was done in a state of self-induced intoxication it will be no defence if the crime is one of basic intent within *DPP* v *Majewski* [1977] AC 142.

- Note other self-induced situations:
  - *R* v *Bailey* [1983] 1 WLR 760

4. Intoxication

a) It includes a state of mind induced by drugs

- *R* v *Lipman* [1970] 1 QB 152

b) If it causes a disease of mind, the defence is insanity

c) It may enable D to establish a mistake of fact incompatible with criminal responsibility

- *A–G for Northern Ireland* v *Gallagher* [1963] AC 349
- *Jaggard* v *Dickinson* [1981] QB 527

d) It may negative the specific intent required in an offence. Note self-induced intoxication may be a defence to a specific intent crime although it cannot be a defence to a basic intent crime.

- *DPP* v *Majewski*, above
- *R* v *Hardie* [1985] 1 WLR 64

Involuntary intoxication may be a defence to either type of crime so long as it negatives mens rea.

- *MPC* v *Caldwell* [1982] AC 341
- *R* v *Lipman* [1970] 1 QB 152
- *R* v *Kingston* [1994] 3 WLR 519 HL
- *R* v *Davies (Leslie)* [1983] Crim LR 741

e) Apart from the above circumstances intoxication is irrelevant.

- *A-G for Northern Ireland* v *Gallagher*, above

5. Mistake

a) This is a defence if:

- D's conduct would not have been a crime had the facts been as he mistakenly believed them to be:
  - *Albert* v *Lavin* [1981] 1 All ER 628

- It negatives the particular mens rea necessary to prove the crime charged:
  - *DPP* v *Morgan* [1976] AC 182
  - *R* v *Tolson* (1889) 23 QBD 168
  - *R* v *Smith* [1974] QB 354

b) Mistake of law

- Ignorance of the law is no defence.
- A mistake as to the civil law, or D's legal rights, may negative mens rea.
  - *R* v *Smith*, above

6. Necessity

a) This is a plea that D's intentional conduct which would otherwise be criminal was not criminal because what he did was necessary to avoid a greater evil.

b) Generally the English law does not recognise such a defence.

- *R* v *Dudley & Stephens* (1884) 14 QBD 273
- *Buckoke* v *GLC* [1971] 2 All ER 254

But see:

- *R* v *Willer* (1986) 83 Cr App R 225
- *R* v *Martin* (1988) 88 Cr App R 343
- *R* v *Conway* [1988] 3 All ER 1025
- *R* v *Pommell* (1995) 2 Cr App R 607

c) In certain circumstances an offence may be defined in such a way that necessity does provide a defence, eg Abortion Act 1967, Criminal Damage Act 1971, self-defence, s3 Criminal Law Act 1967.

7. Self defence

There is a considerable overlap between the right to use reasonable force to prevent crime (see s3 Criminal Law Act

1967) and the right to use reasonable force in self-defence (see *R* v *Oatridge* [1992] Crim LR 205).

- *Palmer* v *R* [1971] AC 814 PC
- *R* v *Clegg* [1995] 2 WLR 80 HL
- *R* v *Owino* [1995] Crim LR 743

8. Duress

a) D must have committed the offence only because of a threat of death or serious personal injury.

- *DPP for Northern Ireland* v *Lynch* [1975] AC 653

b) The threat must be:

- Immediate
  - *R* v *Hudson & Taylor* [1971] 2 QB 202
- Need not be to the accused
  - *R* v *Hurley & Murray* [1967] VR 526
- Such that on the basis of what the defendant reasonably believed was said or done to him, he had good cause to fear that, if he did not so act, he would be killed and/or suffer serious physical injury and that a sober person of reasonable firmness, sharing the defendant's characteristics would have responded to whatever he reasonably believed was said or done by taking part in the crime.
  - *R* v *Howe* [1987] AC 417
  - *R* v *Graham* (1982) 74 Cr App R 235
  - *R* v *Bowen* (1996) 2 Cr App R 157
  - *R* v *Flatt* [1996] Crim LR 576
- The fact that D's will to resist had been eroded by voluntary consumption of drink or drugs is irrelevant.
- Duress of circumstances
  - *R* v *Conway* [1988] 3 All ER 1025

– *R* v *Martin* (1988) 88 Cr App R 343

– *R* v *Hegarty* [1994] Crim LR 353

c) The defence applies to all crimes except murder and attempted murder.

- *R* v *Howe*, above
- *Abbott* v *R* [1977] AC 755
- *R* v *Gotts* [1992] 2 AC 412

Note it is no longer available as a defence to a secondary party to murder and *DPP for Northern Ireland* v *Lynch* (1975) above has been overruled by *R* v *Howe*, above.

9. Marital coercion

a) Section 47 Criminal Justice Act 1925 replaces the common law presumption of marital coercion.

b) On a charge against a wife for any offence, other than murder or treason, it shall be a defence for the wife to prove that the offence was committed in the presence of and under the coercion of her husband.

- *R* v *Richman and Richman* [1982] Crim LR 507
- *R* v *Shortland* [1995] Crim LR 893

Sample Question

'When the courts take into account the particular propensities of a defendant when considering the defence of duress they refuse to do so when considering objective recklessness. Such a distinction is, however, unjustifiable.'

Discuss.

Further Reading

- HLT Textbook Chapters 13, 14 and 15
- Law Commission Report No 229 (1995) on intoxication and criminal liability
- Gardner 'Criminal Defences by Judicial Discretion: *R* v *Kingston*' (1995) 111 LQR 177

- Gough 'Intoxication and Criminal Liability' the Law Commission's Proposed Reforms' (1996) 112 LQR 335
- Horder 'Law Commission on Intoxication' (1995) 58 MLR 534
- Jefferson 'Duress of Circumstances' (1996) 30 LTeach 208
- Jones 'Insanity, Automatism and the Burden of Proof on the Accused' (1995) 111 LQR 475
- Padfield 'Duress, Necessity and the Law Commission' [1993] Crim LR 778
- Smith 'Reshaping the Criminal Law in the House of Lords: *C* v *DPP*' [1995] CLJ 486
- Spencer 'Involuntary Intoxication as a Defence: *R* v *Kingston*' [1995] CLJ 12

TOPIC 8: Theft and Related Offences

1. Theft

Theft involves a dishonest appropriation of property belonging to another with intent to permanently deprive: s1(1) Theft Act (TA) 1968.

Appropriation: s3(1) TA 1968

a) Any assumption of the rights of the owner including where D comes by the property without stealing it, any later assumption of a right to it by keeping or dealing with it as owner.

b) It is not necessary to show that D's act is unauthorised to prove appropriation.

- *Lawrence* v *Metropolitan Police Commissioner* [1972] AC 626
- *Dobson* v *General Accident Fire & Life Assurance Corp plc* [1989] 3 All ER 927
- *R* v *Gomez* [1992] 3 WLR 1067 HL
- *R* v *Mazo* [1996] Crim LR 435

c) Any assumption of any of the owner's rights is sufficient.

- *R* v *Morris* [1983] 3 WLR 697

d) D must be dishonest at the time of the appropriation.

e) Note the limited protection provided in s3(2) to a bona fide purchaser who will not be guilty of theft by any later assumption of rights on the owner.

- *R* v *Adams* [1993] Crim LR 72

Property: s4(1) Theft Act 1968

a) It includes money and all other property real or personal including things in action and other intangible property, but does not include land.

b) Note electricity is not intangible property, nor is confidential information.

- *Low* v *Blease* (1975) 119 SJ 695
- *Oxford* v *Moss* [1979] Crim LR 119

c) Land cannot be stolen, nor can things forming part of it or severed from it except:

- where D is a trustee or personal representative or otherwise authorised to dispose of another's land, he appropriates the land or things forming part of it by dealing with it in an unauthorised way; or
- where he is not in possession of the land, he severs anything forming part of the land, or causes it to be severed; or
- where he is a tenant, he appropriates the whole or part of any fixture or structure let to be used with the land: s4(2).

d) Note the provisions of s4(3) and s4(4) regarding the picking of wild mushrooms etc (s4(3)) and poaching (s4(4)).

Belonging to another: s5(1) TA 1968

a) Property is regarded as belonging to a person having possession, control or a proprietary right in it (other than an equitable interest arising out of an agreement to transfer or grant an interest).

- *R* v *Turner (No 2)* [1971] 2 All ER 441
- *R* v *Meredith* [1973] Crim LR 253
- *Attorney-General Reference (No 2 of 1982)* [1984] 2 All ER 216
- *R* v *Bonner* [1970] 1 WLR 838

b) Trust property belongs to any person who may enforce the trust (s5(2)).

c) Where a person receives property from another and is under a legal obligation to deal with it or its proceeds in a particular way, the property is regarded as belonging to another (s5(3)).

- *R* v *Hall* [1973] QB 126
- *R* v *Mainwairing* (1981) 74 Cr App R 99
- *Davidge* v *Bunnett* [1984] Crim LR 296
- *Attorney-General's Reference (No 1 of 1985)* [1986] QB 491
- *R* v *Wills* (1991) 92 Cr App R 297
- *R* v *Wain* (1995) 2 Cr App R 660

d) Where property is acquired by another's mistake and D is under a legal obligation to make restoration in whole or part of it, then to the extent of that obligation, the property is deemed to belong to another (s5(4)).

- *Moynes* v *Cooper* [1956] 1 QB 439
- *R* v *Gilks* [1972] 3 All ER 280

Mens rea

a) The defendant must be *dishonest*

- Note that s2 TA 1968 gives a partial definition of dishonesty in that it states that a person does not act dishonestly in certain circumstances eg when he believes he has a claim of right (s2(1)(a)); he believes that the owner would have consented (s2(1)(b)); or he believes that the owner cannot be discovered on taking reasonable steps (s2(1)(c)).
  - *R* v *Holden* [1991] Crim LR 478

  The dishonest intent must be formed while the goods belong to another.
- D may be dishonest notwithstanding that he is willing to pay for the property: s2(2).
- Apart from cases specifically covered in s2 it is for the jury to decide if D acted dishonestly and two questions must be considered:

Was D's act dishonest according to the ordinary standards of reasonable and honest people? If yes:

Did D realise that what he was doing was by those standards dishonest? If yes, he is dishonest.

- *R* v *Feely* [1973] 1 QB 530
- *R* v *Ghosh* [1982] 1 QB 1053

b) Intention to permanently deprive

- The element of permanence relates to the deprivation of the victim, not the proposed benefit to D.
- Certain states of mind may be equivalent to an intention to permanently deprive and these are noted in s6 which seeks to clarify the meaning of the phrase in certain respects:
  - Section 6(1): a person who appropriates another's property without meaning the other permanently to lose it, is to be regarded as having an intention to permanently deprive if he intends to treat it as his own to dispose of regardless of the other's rights, and a borrowing or lending may amount to so treating it if it is for a period and in circumstances that amount to an outright taking or disposal.
  - Section 6(2): where a person in possession or control of another's property parts with it under a condition which he may not be able to perform, this may amount to treating the property as his own regardless of the other's rights.
  - *R* v *Downes* [1983] Crim LR 819
  - *R* v *Lloyd* [1985] QB 829
  - *R* v *Fernandes* [1996] 1 Cr App R 175
  - *R* v *Easom* [1971] 2 QB 315
  - *Attorney-General's References (Nos 1 & 2 of 1979)* [1979] 2 WLR 578
  - *R* v *Velumyl* [1989] Crim LR 299

2. Robbery

a) Where D steals and immediately before or at the time of doing so, and in order to do so, he uses force on any person, or puts or seeks to put any person in fear of being then and there subjected to force.

- Section 8 TA 1968

b) D must be guilty of theft.

c) Force must be directed against a person, not necessarily the victim. Note the meaning of 'force'.

- *R* v *Dawson* [1976] Crim LR 692
- *R* v *Clouden* [1987] Crim LR 56

d) Force must be used 'immediately before or at the time of stealing', and be used 'in order to' steal.

- *R* v *Hale* (1978) 68 Cr App R 415
- *R* v *Shendley* [1970] Crim LR 49

3. Burglary

a) D is guilty of burglary where:

- he enters a building or part of a building as a trespasser with intent to steal, inflict GBH on any person therein, commit rape or do unlawful damage (s9(1)(a) TA 1968); or
- having entered a building or part of a building as a trespasser he steals or attempts to steal, or inflicts or attempts to inflict GBH on any person therein (s9(1)(b)).

b) The entry must be a trespass and be substantial and effective.

- *R* v *Collins* [1972] 2 All ER 1105; [1973] QB 100
- *R* v *Brown* (1985) The Times 31 January; [1985] Crim LR 212
- *R* v *Laing* [1995] Crim LR 395
- *R* v *Ryan* [1996] Crim LR 320

c) The entry must be to a building or part of a building.

- *R* v *Walkington* (1978) 68 Cr App R 427

d) Mens rea

Under s9(1) D must enter the building as a trespasser ie he must know or be reckless as to the facts which make his entry trespassory.

- *R* v *Collins*, above

Note the ulterior intents in s9(1)(a) and s9(1)(b)

- *A-G's References (Nos 1 & 2 of 1979)*, above

4. Aggravated burglary

a) Where D commits burglary and at the time has with him any firearm, imitation firearm, any weapon of offence, or an explosive: s10 TA 1968.

b) Where the alleged burglary falls under s9(1)(a) it must be shown that D had the weapon of offence with him at the time of entry. Where the burglary falls under s9(1)(b) D has to have the weapon with him at the time he commits the ulterior offence.

- *R* v *Kelly* (1992) 97 Cr App R 245

5. Removal of an article from a place open to the public

a) Where the public have access to a building in order to view the building or part of it, or a collection or part of it housed therein, any person who without lawful authority removes from the building or grounds the whole or part of an article displayed or kept for display in the building or that part of it, or the grounds, shall commit an offence: s11 TA 1968.

b) There must be a building to which the public have access in order to view.

- *R* v *Barr* [1978] Crim LR 244

c) Commercial exhibitions are not covered.

d) The article removed must be displayed or kept for display to the public.

e) 'Collection' includes a collection got together for temporary purposes.

f) Where the public have access for a limited period anything removed which does not form part of a collection kept permanently for display, must be removed on a day when the public have access.

g) No offence is committed where D believes he has lawful authority to remove the article, or that the owner would have consented to the removal: s11(3) TA 1968.

6. Taking a motor vehicle or other conveyance without authority

a) If, without having the owner's consent, or other lawful authority, D takes a conveyance for his own or another's use, or knowing it has been taken without authority, drives it or allows himself to be carried in it, he is guilty of an offence: s12 TA 1968.

b) Conveyance

Any conveyance constructed or adapted for the carriage of a person by land, sea or air: s12(7) TA 1968.

c) Taking

- There must be some movement.
  - *R* v *Bogacki* [1973] QB 832
  - *R* v *Diggin* [1980] Crim LR 656
- It must be for one's own or another's use as a conveyance
  - *R* v *Bow* (1976) 64 Cr App R 54
  - *R* v *Stokes* [1982] Crim LR 695
  - *R* v *Pearce* [1973] Crim LR 321
- It must be without the owner's consent or other lawful authority.
  - *McKnight* v *Davies* [1974] RTR 4
  - *R* v *Wibberley* [1966] 2 QB 214

  - *R* v *Peart* [1970] 2 QB 672
  - *Whittaker* v *Campbell* [1983] 3 WLR 676

d) No offence is committed if D believes he has lawful authority to take the conveyance, or he believes he would have had the owner's consent if he knew of the circumstances: s12(6) TA 1968.

  - *R* v *Clotworthy* [1981] Crim LR 501
  - *R* v *Gannon* (1988) 87 Cr App R 254

e) Note s12A TA 1968 – aggravated vehicle taking:

  - D must commit an offence under s12(1) in respect of a *mechanically propelled vehicle* (s12A(1)(a)); and
  - At any time after vehicle unlawfully taken by D or another, and before it is recovered, the vehicle was driven or injury or damage was caused in one of the circumstances set out in s12A(2)(a), (b), (c) or (d) (s12A(1)(b)).
  - D *not* guilty if he proves that the driving, injury, damage happened before he committed the s12(1) offence or that he was not in nor on nor in the immediate vicinity of the vehicle when the driving, accident or damage occurred: s12A(3) TA 1968.

f) Note that a summary offence of taking a pedal cycle is created by s12(5) TA 1968.

g) Note the provisions of s9 Criminal Attempts Act 1981 in respect of interference with a motor vehicle or trailer or anything carried therein.

7. Abstracting electricity

a) Where a person dishonestly uses, without due authority, or dishonestly causes to be wasted or diverted any electricity, he commits an offence: s13 TA 1968.

b) Note: electricity is not property for the purposes of stealing.

  - *Low* v *Blease* (1975) 119 SJ 695

c) Dishonesty will be tested according to *R* v *Ghosh* [1982] 1 QB 1053.

8. Obtaining property by deception

a) Where a person by any deception, dishonestly obtains property belonging to another with intent to permanently deprive the other of it, he commits an offence: s15(1) TA 1968.

b) Obtains

Means to obtain ownership, possession or control of it, and includes obtaining for another, or enabling another to retain: s15(2).

c) Deception

- Means any deception (deliberate or reckless) by words or conduct as to fact or law, including a deception as to the present intentions of the deceiver or any other person: s15(4).
- D may deceive by conduct.
  - *R* v *Barnard* (1837) 7 C and P 784
  - *DPP* v *Ray* [1974] AC 370
  - *R* v *Coady* [1996] Crim LR 518 (CA)
- It is not possible to deceive a machine, the deception must operate on a human mind.
  - *Davies* v *Flackett* (1972) 116 SJ 526
- Note the representations made in the use of cheques and cheque and credit card.
  - *R* v *Lambie* [1981] 1 All ER 332
- The deception must precede the obtaining, and be the cause of the obtaining.
  - *R* v *Collis-Smith* [1971] Crim LR 716
  - *R* v *Clucas* [1949] 2 KB 226
  - *R* v *Rashid* [1977] 2 All ER 237

  - *R* v *Doukas* [1978] 1 All ER 1061
  - *R* v *King and Stockwell* [1987] Crim LR 398
  - But note: *R* v *Miller* [1992] Crim LR 744

d) Property belonging to another

The definition of property in s4(1) TA 1968 applies to a s15 offence. Note, however, that land is capable of being obtained by deception.

- Decision in *R* v *Preddy* [1996] 3 WLR 255 (HL), which was reversed by Theft Amendment Act below.
- Section 1 of the Theft (Amendment) Act 1996, which inserts a 15A into the Theft Act 1968 creates a new offence of obtaining a money transfer by deception. This reverses the decision in *R* v *Preddy* [1996] 3 All ER 481 where the HL held that although the appellants had obtained mortgages by giving false information, the transfer of money between bank accounts was not illegal because no 'property' had passed from the payer to the payee.
- Section 2 of the 1996 Act inserts s1(3) into the Theft Act 1978, which includes the making of a loan within the definition of a service for the offence of obtaining services by deception (reversing *R* v *Halai* [1983] Crim LR 624).

e) Mens rea

- Intentional or reckless (*R* v *Cunningham* [1982] AC 566) deception
- Intention to obtain property
- The test of dishonesty to be applied is that in *Ghosh*, above
- Section 6(1) Theft Act 1968 applies to s15 with regard to 'intention to permanently deprive': s15(3).
  - *R* v *Mitchell* [1993] Crim LR 788 – overruled by *R* v *Preddy*, above

– *R* v *Caresana* [1996] Crim LR 667 (CA)

– *R* v *Graham (HK)* (1996) The Times 28 October (CA)

9. Obtaining pecuniary advantage by deception

a) Where a person by any deception dishonestly obtains a pecuniary advantage he shall commit an offence: s16(1) Theft Act 1968.

b) Pecuniary advantage

This is defined in s16(2)(b) and s16(2)(c):

- He is allowed to borrow by way of overdraft or to take out an insurance or annuity contract or obtain an improvement of terms on the same: s16(2)(b).

  – *R* v *Lambie*, above

- He is given the opportunity to earn a remuneration or greater remuneration in an office or employment or to win money by betting: s16(2)(c).

  – *R* v *Clucas* [1949] 2 KB 226

c) Deception

See discussion under s15 above.

d) Dishonesty

The test is according to *Ghosh*, above

10. False accounting

Where D dishonestly, with a view to gain for himself or another, or with intent to cause loss to another, destroys, defaces, conceals or falsifies any account or record or document made for accounting purposes, or produces or makes use of any such document or account which he knows is misleading, false or deceptive in a material particular, he commits an offence: s17 Theft Act 1968.

- *Edwards* v *Toombs* [1983] Crim LR 43

11. Offences under the Theft Act 1978

Obtaining services by deception: s1

a) Where any person by a deception dishonestly obtains services from another, he shall be guilty: s1(1).

b) The other must be induced to confer a benefit by doing an act or causing or permitting some act to be done on the understanding the benefit has or will be paid for: s1(2).

c) Deception has the same meaning as under s15.

d) The definition of services is wide and they do not have to be legally enforceable, but they must be performed on the understanding that payment has been or will be made.

- *R* v *Halai* [1983] Crim LR 624
- *R* v *Shortland* [1995] Crim LR 893

e) Dishonesty is tested according to *Ghosh,* above.

Evasion of liability by deception: s2(1)

a) D by deception dishonestly secures the remission of the whole or part of any existing liability to make payment, whether his own or another's liability: s2(1)(a), eg D gets his creditor to agree he will never seek payment. Quaere: how is 'secured' to be construed?

- *R* v *Jackson* [1983] Crim R 617

b) D, with intent to make permanent default, in whole or part of an existing liability, or to let another do so, dishonestly induces the creditor to wait for payment or forgo payment: s2(1)(b). This is concerned with the 'stalling' of debtors and is probably the widest of the three changes under s2.

- *R* v *Attewell-Hughes* (1991) 93 Cr App R 132
- Payment by cheque or other security is treated as being induced to wait for payment: s2(3).

c) D dishonestly obtained any exemption of abatement of liability: s2(1)(c).

- Includes prospective liabilities as well as existing ones.
- It covers reductions and exemptions from liability and would cover obtaining allowances or rebates.
  - *R* v *Sibartie* [1983] Crim LR 470

d) Section 2 is limited to legally enforceable liabilities.

e) Dishonesty is tested according to *Ghosh,* above.

Making off without payment

a) D, knowing that payment on the spot for any goods supplied or service done is required or expected from him, dishonestly makes off without having paid as expected or required, with intent to avoid payment: s3 Theft Act 1978.

b) Section 3 does not apply to transactions where the supply of goods or doing of a service is *contrary to the law*; or where payment for the service done is not *legally enforceable*: s3(3).

c) Payment on the spot

D must know payment then and there is required or expected of him.

- *R* v *Brooks and Brooks* (1982) 76 Cr App R 66

d) Note examples of the situation where s3 will apply.

- *R* v *Collis-Smith* [1971] Crim LR 716

e) Dishonestly makes off

Dishonesty does not have to be present at the time when the goods are supplied or service is done. It has to be present when D 'makes off'.

- *R* v *McDavitt* [1981] Crim LR 843

f) Without payment

g) With intent to avoid payment

D must intend to avoid payment altogether.

- *R* v *Allen* [1985] AC 1029

h) Payment must be required or expected

- *Troughton* v *Metropolitan Police* [1987] Crim LR 138

12. Blackmail

a) D, with a view to gain for himself or another, or with intent to cause loss to another, makes any unwarranted demand with menaces and a demand is unwarranted unless made in the belief:

- That he has reasonable grounds for making it, and
- That the use of the menaces is a proper means of enforcing the demand: s21 Theft Act 1968.

b) Makes any demand

Can be made orally or in writing or in some other way and may be express or implied. A demand is made by letter when the letter is posted.

- *Treacy* v *DPP* [1971] AC 537

c) Menaces

'Threats of action detrimental or unpleasant to the person addressed'

- *Thorne* v *Motor Trade Association* [1937] AC 797
- *R* v *Clear* [1968] 1 QB 670
- *R* v *Garwood* [1987] 1 All ER 1032

d) Mens rea

A demand is *unwarranted* unless:

- D believes he has reasonable grounds for making the demand; and

  D believes that the use of the menaces is a proper means of reinforcing that demand.
- The burden of proof. D bears an evidential burden to show he held *both* beliefs.
  - *R* v *Lawrence* (1971) 57 Cr App R 64
- The test is subjective
  - *R* v *Harvey* (1980) 72 Cr App R 139

D must have a view to gain, or intend to cause loss to another.

- 'Gain' includes a gain by keeping what one has, as well as a gain by getting what one has not.

- 'Loss' includes not getting what one might get and parting with what one has: s34(2).
  - *R* v *Parkes* [1973] Crim LR 358

13. Handling stolen goods

a) D otherwise than in the course of stealing, knowing or believing the goods to be stolen, dishonestly receives stolen goods or dishonestly undertakes or assists in their retention, removal, disposal or realisation by or for the benefit of another person, or he arranges to do so: s22 Theft Act 1968.

b) Stolen goods

- 'Goods' include money and every other description of property except land, but includes things severed from the land by stealing: s34(2)(b).
- 'Stolen' means stolen contrary to s1 Theft Act 1968, or obtained by deception contrary to s15 Theft Act 1968, or obtained by blackmail: s24 Theft Act 1968.
- Proceeds of the original theft may become stolen goods if they directly or indirectly represent or have at any time so represented the stolen goods in the hands of a thief or a handler: s24(2).
  - *Attorney-General's Reference (No 4 of 1979)* (1980) 71 Cr App R 341
- Goods cease to be stolen when they are restored to the owner or to other lawful possession, or after the owner has ceased to have rights of restitution: s24(3).
  - *R* v *King and Stockwell* [1987] Crim LR 398
  - *A-G's Reference (No 1 of 1974)* [1974] 1 QB 744
  - *Haughton* v *Smith* [1975] AC 476

c) Note the forms of handling and that in relation to undertaking or assisting in the retention, removal etc, the acts must be done 'by or for the benefit of another person'.

- *R* v *Bloxham* [1982] 1 All ER 582

d) Can handling be committed by omission?

- *R* v *Brown* [1970] 1 QB 105
- *R* v *Pitchley* (1973) 57 Cr App R 30

e) Note the overlap with theft.

- *R* v *Cash* [1985] Crim LR 311

f) Mens rea

- D must know or believe the goods to be stolen – mere suspicion is not sufficient.
  - *R* v *Grainge* [1974] 1 All ER 928
- Note the provisions of s27(3) Theft Act 1968 regarding proof of this element of mens rea.
- Dishonesty is tested according to *Ghosh* above, but note *R* v *Roberts* [1986] Crim LR 122
  - *R* v *Brennan* [1990] Crim LR 118

14. Going equipped for stealing

a) D when not in his place of abode has with him any article for use in the course of or in connection with any burglary, theft or cheat: s25 Theft Act 1968.

b) It includes an article made or adapted for such use.

c) 'Cheat' means obtaining property by deception.

d) It has to be shown that the article was for the use in connection with the theft or cheat. But it is sufficient to show that D intended to use it if the opportunity arose.

- *R* v *Rashid* [1977] 2 All ER 237
- *R* v *Doukas* [1978] 1 All ER 1061
- *R* v *Hargreaves* [1985] Crim LR 243
- *R* v *Cooke* [1986] AC 909
- *R* v *Goodwin* [1996] Crim LR 262

Sample Questions

1. While shopping in a supermarket, Peter picked up a bottle of wine and put it under his jacket intending to leave the shop without paying for it. Before he left the shop he noticed someone whom he believed was a store detective watching him and he put the bottle of wine in a shopping basket and paid for it at the checkout. Jenny, a cashier in the same supermarket, took £30 from the till to give to her friend Barney to place a bet on a horse racing in the 2.30 at Epsom. Jenny intended to repay the money before she finished her shift. Unfortunately, although the horse she instructed Barney to place the bet on won the race, Barney had spent the £30 which Jenny had given him on buying his friends drinks in a public house rather than using it to place the bet. Later that day a customer bought goods costing £14.50 and gave Jenny a £20 note. Jenny, who was thinking about what she would have spent her winnings on thought that the customer had given her £50 and gave the customer £35.50 change. When the customer subsequently met his friends for a drink, he discovered the mistake and said to his friends, 'that bloody fool in the supermarket gave me too much change, the drinks are on me'.

   Advise Peter, Jenny and the customer as to their criminal liability, if any.
2. Kay has an account with Bunkley's bank and has a cheque guarantee card which guarantees payment on her cheques up to £50. Kay has been overdrawn for the last two months and has received repeated warnings from the bank to stop issuing cheques. Kay uses a cheque with a guarantee card to buy herself a pair of shoes for £35 from the A&C Department Store. She also buys a winter coat as a birthday present for her mother for £96 using another cheque which the assistant accepts because he recognises Kay as a regular customer. The bank honours the cheque for £35 but refuses to do so for the other cheque marking it 'return to drawer'. Before Kay leaves the shop she sees a gold bracelet with 'M Twaine' stencilled on it. She looks around but cannot see who might have dropped it and takes it home intending to sell it.

   Advise Kay as to her criminal liability, if any.

3. Consider the criminal liability of Jane in the following situations:

   a) Jane attempts to wrench V's watch from the latter's wrist but fails to do so when V pushes her away;

   b) Jane snatches V's bag which V has put on the ground beside him. After snatching V's bag and while about to run off V grabs Jane who then punches V in the face in order to make her escape.

4. Discuss the criminal liability of the accused in the following situations:

   a) Alfred, a law student at the London Goldhall University is walking in the corridor of his university when he notices the window of his lecturers office open. He reaches inside and steals a copy of *Smith and Hogan on Criminal Law* from the desk adjacent to the window.

      Would it make any difference to your answer if Alfred's arm was not long enough to reach the book and after trying to do so he left empty handed?

   b) Mary's lecturer in contract law asks her to come into his office to discuss an essay. Mary enters the office but after a few moments the lecturer is called out of the office for a short while. Mary saw that her lecturer had left his wallet on the table, took it and put it in her pocket. Later that day the lecturer asked Mary about his missing wallet but Mary denied all knowledge of it.

      Would it make any difference to your answer if Mary had seen the wallet in an area of the office used by another lecturer who shared the office which was separated by the positioning of bookshelves?

   c) At 4am James used a crowbar to force open a window on the ground floor of the university of which he was a student intending to look around and steal anything which he thought he could sell in order to repay some of his overdraft. James left the crowbar near the window but after walking further down the corridor upon hearing a noise and thinking it might be a security guard picked up a hammer which a contractor had left lying around. Finding nothing which he thought he could sell James left the premises empty handed and without encountering any guards.

Would it make any difference to your answer if:

i) As he was about to leave James stole some books which he found piled up in the corridor?

ii) He smashed a door to gain entry to the audio-visual room and stole a video recorder?

Further Reading

- HLT Textbook Chapters 16–23 (on theft and related offences)
- Gardner 'Appropriation in Theft: the Last Word?' (1993) 109 LQR 194
- Glazebrook 'Revising the Theft Acts' [1993] CLJ 191
- Shute and Horder 'Thieving and Deceiving: What is the Difference?' (1993) 56 MLR 548
- Spencer 'The Aggravated Vehicle Taking Act 1992' [1992] Crim LR 699

TOPIC 9: Forgery and Counterfeiting; Perjury

1. Forgery and Counterfeiting

a) D makes a false instrument with intention that he or another shall use it to induce someone to accept it as genuine, and by reason of such acceptance, to do or not to do some act to his own or another's prejudice: s1 Forgery and Counterfeiting Act 1981.

- Note also the further offences in ss2, 3 and 4 (copying, using and using a copy of a false instrument).

b) Actus reus

- It is complete as soon as D makes a false instrument.
- 'Instrument' means any document, any stamp issued or sold by the Post Office; any Inland Revenue stamp, any disc, tape, soundtrack or other device on or in which information is recorded or stored by mechanical, electronic or other means: s8.
- Note the definition of when an instrument will be false under the Act in s9.
  - *R* v *Hassard and Devereaux* [1970] 2 All ER 647
  - *R* v *Donelly* (1984) 79 Cr App R 76
  - *R* v *Moore* [1987] 3 All ER 825

c) Mens rea

- Section 10 defines 'induce' and 'prejudice' in detail.
  - *R* v *Campbell (Mary)* [1984] Crim LR 683
  - *R* v *Parker* (1910) 74 JP 210
- D must know the document is false and must intend that it be used by himself or another to induce someone to accept it as genuine and on doing so to act to his own or another's prejudice.

d) • Under s14 it is an offence to make a counterfeit of a currency note or of a protected coin intending that he or another shall pass or tender it as genuine: s14(1).

It is also an offence to make a counterfeit of a currency note or of a protected coin without lawful authority or excuse: s14(2).

• Sections 15, 16 and 17 create offences of passing counterfeit notes and coins, having custody or control of them and having custody or control of materials for making them.

• Section 18 prohibits the reproduction of a British currency note without written consent and s19 prohibits the making, sale or distribution of such imitation without written consent.

2. Perjury

a) D, who is lawfully sworn as a witness in judicial proceedings, wilfully makes a material statement knowing it to be false, or not believing it to be true: s1 Perjury Act 1911

b) Lawfully sworn

Where D swears by God according to his religion which need not be Christian. He may affirm without giving reason.

c) Judicial proceedings

Includes proceedings before any court, tribunal or person lawfully empowered to receive evidence on oath.

d) Statement

May be as to fact or opinion. D may be liable even if it is true, if he believed it to be false or was reckless as to whether it was true or false.

e) Materiality

Statements are material if they relate to the outcome of the proceedings, the credibility of a witness or the question of punishment.

- *R* v *Millward* [1985] 1 All ER 859

f) Mens rea

Involves an intention to make a statement, knowledge or belief that it is false, or reckless as to whether it is true or false. Objective negligence is *not* sufficient, and a positive belief in the truth of a statement is a defence.

Sample Questions

1. Explain, referring to relevant cases, the rule, in forgery, that 'the document must not only tell a lie, but also it must tell a lie about itself'.
2. Robin was called as a witness for the prosecution in an affray case. His evidence was to be about what he saw of the fighting in a dance hall. In the opening questions of the examination-in-chief, prosecuting counsel asked Robin about his age, address and occupation. Robin answered that he was 30 years old, lived in the city and was a bank manager.

   The questioning then turned to the events of the night of the fight. Robin was not in fact a bank manager, but was only a cashier in the bank.

   Has he committed perjury?

Further Reading

- HLT Textbook Chapters 24 and 25

TOPIC 10: Strict, Vicarious and Corporate Liability

1. Strict liability

a) These offences may be committed even though as regards one or more important elements of the offence, D has no means rea.

b) Distinguish strict liability from absolute liability.

- *R* v *Prince* (1875) LR 2 CCR 154
- *R* v *Hibbert* (1869) LR 1 CCR 184
- *R* v *Larsonneur* (1933) 149 LT 542

c) Most strict liability offences are the creation of statute and whether a statute requires or dispenses with mens rea is a question of construction.

- *Sherras* v *De Rutzen* [1895] 1 QB 918
- *R* v *Blake* (1996) The Times 14 August (CA)

d) Note the areas in which strict liability offences have been created, eg:

- Inflation
- Drugs
  - *Warner* v *MPC* [1969] 2 AC 256
  - but note *Sweet* v *Parsley* [1970] AC 132
- Pollution
  - *Alphacell* v *Woodward* [1972] AC 824

e) It has been argued that it would be better to replace strict liability offences with offences where liability would be dependent on negligence.

f) Note the tendency to restrict strict liability to regulatory or 'quasi-criminal' offences.

- *Sweet* v *Parsley*, above

2. Vicarious liability

a) This doctrine fixes liability on X for acts committed by Y, but unlike tort there is no general principle of vicarious liability in criminal law.

b) Public nuisance is the only common law offence involving vicarious liability.

c) Vicarious liability has been imposed in two distinct situations as exceptions to the general rule that a master is not liable for the acts of his accomplice unless he is an accomplice:

- Where a person has delegated to another the performance of duties imposed on him by law.
  - *Allen* v *Whitehead* [1930] 1 KB 211
  - *Vane* v *Yiannopoullous* [1965] AC 486
  - *Howker* v *Robinson* [1973] 1 QB 178
  - *R* v *Winson* [1969] 1 QB 371
- Where in law the physical acts of the servant are deemed to be the master's acts.
  - *Coppen* v *Moore (No 2)* [1898] 2 QB 306
  - *Griffiths* v *Studebakers Ltd* [1924] 1 KB 102
  - *Linnett* v *MPC* [1946] KB 290

d) There can be no vicarious liability for attempts or aiding and abetting offences.

- *Ferguson* v *Weaving* [1951] 1 KB 814

3. Corporate liability

a) A corporation has an identity separate from that of persons who comprise the corporation.

b) It may be subjected to criminal liability in two ways:

- By using the doctrine of vicarious liability, but note:
  - *R* v *ICR Haulage Co Ltd* [1944] KB 551

- By using the 'alter ego' theory ie there are certain persons who direct the affairs of the company, and when they are acting on company business they are regarded as the company.
  - *Tesco* v *Nattrass* [1972] AC 153
  - *Moore* v *Bresler* [1944] 2 All ER 515
  - *Meridian Global Funds Management Asia* v *Securities Commission* [1995] 3 WLR 413

c) The 'alter ego' theory does not apply to crimes not punishable by fines eg murder, and crimes of a personal nature eg rape, bigamy, perjury; or to conspiracy if only one of its directive staff is involved and there are no other co-conspirators. But note: *R* v *Coroner for East Kent ex parte Spooner* (1989) 88 Cr App R 10 in which Bingham LJ was prepared to accept that a corporate body could be guilty of manslaughter where both the actus reus and mens rea could be established against those who were the 'embodiment of the corporate body itself'.

Sample Questions

1. What criteria do the courts employ when deciding whether a statute gives rise to strict liability? Illustrate your answer with appropriate authorities.
2. Explain the circumstances in which a corporation may be criminally liable, and discuss whether such liability involves injustice.

Further Reading

- HLT Textbook Chapter 25
- Cartwright 'Defendants in Consumer Protection Statutes: A Search for Consistency' (1996) 59 MLR 225
- Clarkson 'Kicking Corporate Bodies and Damning their Souls' (1996) 59 MLR 557
- Grantham 'Corporate Knowledge: Identification or Attribution?' (1996) 59 MLR 732

- Sullivan 'The Attribution of Culpability to Limited Companies' [1996] CLJ 515
- Wells 'Corporate Liability and Consumer Protection: *Tesco* v *Natrass Revisited*' (1994) 57 MLR 817